BIRDS

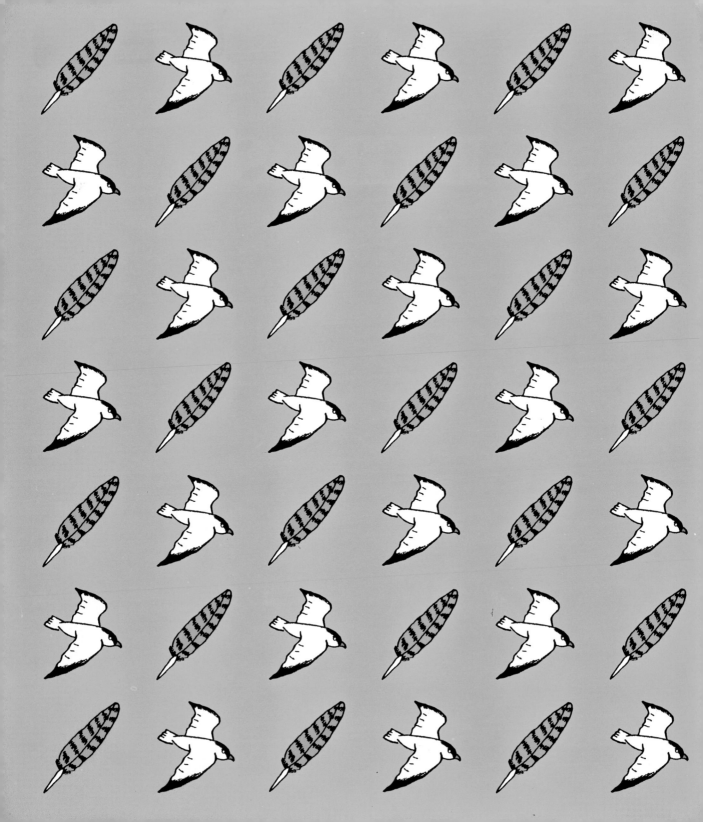

© 1993 Franklin Watts

Franklin Watts, Inc.
95 Madison Avenue
New York, NY 10016

Library of Congress Cataloging-in-Publication Data

Richardson, Joy.
    Birds / by Joy Richardson.
        p. cm. — (Picture science)
    Includes index.
    Summary: An introduction to birds and how they fly,
breathe, and live.
    ISBN 0-531-14262-0
    1. Birds — Juvenile literature. [1. Birds.] I. Title.
    II. Series: Richardson, Joy. Picture science.
    QL676.2.R55 1993
    598—dc20   93-18558
                                                      CIP AC

10 9 8 7 6 5 4 3 2 1

Editor: Sarah Ridley
Designer: Janet Watson
Illustrator: Angela Owen
Picture researcher: Sarah Moule

Photographs: Bruce Coleman Ltd title page,
7, 9, 19, 21, 27; Frank Lane Picture Agency 10,
13, 14, 22, 24; Natural History Photographic
Agency cover, 16.

Printed in Malaysia

PICTURE SCIENCE

BIRDS

Joy Richardson

FRANKLIN WATTS

New York • Chicago • London • Toronto • Sydney

Bird varieties

There are about nine thousand different types of bird.

The largest is an ostrich, which is bigger than a human being.
The smallest is a hummingbird, which is about the size of some butterflies.

Birds come in different sizes
and live in different places,
but their bodies all work
in the same kind of way.

Bones inside

Birds have a lightweight skeleton.
Many of their bones are hollow.

The long backbone is
made up of little bones.
It stretches from tail to skull.
Birds have a very long neck.

Leg bones and wing bones
start from the backbone.

Rib bones curve around to
protect the bird's insides.
Birds have a bony plate on
their front to anchor their
powerful wing muscles.

Covered in feathers

Only birds have feathers.

Feathers grow from little tubes in the bird's skin.

The hollow shaft supports the blade of the feather. This is made up of hundreds of threads, called barbs. Each barb is fastened to its neighbor with tiny hooks, like a zipper.

Birds lose their feathers. New feathers grow to replace them.

Keeping warm

Birds are warm-blooded.
Feathers help to keep their
body warm in cold weather.

Birds have down feathers
beneath their smoothly
overlapping body feathers.
Down feathers are short and fluffy.
They trap warm air
close to the bird's skin.

Muscles under the skin can pull
on the ends of the feathers
to fluff them up and
trap more warm air.

Feather care

Birds spend a lot of time
taking care of their feathers.
This is called preening.

They bathe in water or in
dust to loosen the dirt.

Birds use their beak to
pick out lice and fleas.
They can even bend around
to reach their tail.

Oil from a gland near the tail
is smoothed over the feathers.

Birds comb their beak down each feather
to neatly arrange the barbs.

Taking off

Birds are made for flying.

A bird takes off by jumping
into the air, spreading its wings,
and beating them up and down.

The long wing feathers lie flat
as they push down on the air.
As the wing lifts up, the outer
feathers open to let air through.

The curved shape of the wing
helps to pull the bird upward.

When a bird makes a landing,
it spreads out its wings and
tail like a parachute.

Patterns in the air

Birds fly in different ways.

Many small birds, like the bullfinch,
fly in a wavy line,
flapping their wings fast
and then taking a rest.

Ducks and geese fly straight.
They beat their wings all the time.

Gulls glide overhead, floating
on currents of moving air.

Birds of prey soar and swoop.
Kestrels can hover in the air.

Bullfinch   **Goose**

Long-distance flying

Many birds migrate in winter.
They fly to warmer places where
there will be more food.

Birds of the same type gather
in a huge flock to make
the journey together.

Some geese fly in a "V" shape,
taking turns to lead.
They can fly thousands
of miles without stopping.

Birds are good navigators
but no one is sure how
they find their way.

Building nests

Migrating birds return each spring
to their territory.
Then it is time to start building
a nest and laying eggs.

Nest building is hard work.

Birds make many trips
to collect bits of grass, twigs, moss,
feathers, and even paper or string.
They bind all the pieces together and
make a smooth hollow in the middle.

Swallows build their nest under roofs.
They use hundreds of beakfuls of mud.

Most birds nest in trees and hedges.
Some birds nest on the ground.

Baby birds

The mother bird lays a clutch
of eggs in the nest and sits
on them to keep them warm.

The growing birds feed on
the yolk inside their egg.
After a few weeks they are ready to hatch.
The bird pecks its way through the shell
and slowly cracks the egg open.

Most nest birds hatch with
closed eyes and bare skin.
The parents feed their hungry
babies until they are ready to fly.

Inside a bird's egg

Bird beaks

Most birds catch and carry
all their food with their beak.

Birds have no teeth.
Their beak is shaped to
handle their favorite foods.

Finches crack open nuts and seeds.
Hoopoes snap up insects.
Curlews dig out worms.
Gulls go fishing.

Birds have nostrils in their beak
for breathing and smelling.

Hawks and owls use their claws
when pouncing on their prey.

Curlew

Finch

Kestrel

All kinds of birds

All birds lay eggs.
All birds have feathers.

Some birds never fly.

The ostrich is too heavy
to leave the ground.
Penguins use their wings
as flippers for swimming.

For most birds, flying is easy.

Swifts spend almost all
their time in the air.
They can even fly
while they are asleep.

Index